CLARE CONNERY

Salads

Photography by SIMON WHEELER

THE MASTER CHEFS

TED SMART

CLARE CONNERY is one of Ireland's leading food experts: author, journalist, broadcaster, chef and restaurateur. She has owned her own cookery school, restaurant and delicatessen, and as food correspondent for BBC Northern Ireland for 15 years, she wrote and presented many food programmes, including six series of *Cook with Clare*.

She is the author of a number of books, including *In An Irish Country Kitchen*, *The Salad Book*, *Quick and Easy Salads*, *Store Cupboard Cookery* and *The Irish Cook Book*.

Clare currently runs a food consultancy and catering company from bases in Belfast and London.

CONTENTS

It takes four people to make a salad: a miser to put in the vinegar, a spendthrift to add the oil, a wise man to season it and a madman to toss it.

A ROMAN SAYING

INTRODUCTION

Being the committed salad lover that I am, it wasn't easy
selecting just ten recipes from what, over the years, has
become an extensive repertoire. Eventually, after much
deliberation, I settled on the following, not only because they
are among my favourites, but also because they are quick and
easy to prepare and use fairly basic ingredients, which on the
whole are easy to obtain.

These ten recipes are very versatile and although they are
designed as main course salads, they can easily be converted
into simple first courses or snacks.

These salads are representative of the sort of food I like to eat
at least once a day, not too heavy in content and with very
varied flavours. I hope you will find them fresh and
appetizing to eat and as pretty as a picture to look at.

CAESAR SALAD

2 LARGE HEADS OF COS LETTUCE

GARLIC CROÛTONS
2 GARLIC CLOVES, CRUSHED
5 TABLESPOONS OLIVE OIL
3 SLICES OF WHITE BREAD,
    ABOUT 5 MM/¼ INCH THICK,
    CRUSTS REMOVED

CAESAR DRESSING
2 EGGS
6 TABLESPOONS OLIVE OIL
JUICE OF 1 SMALL LEMON
1 TABLESPOON WORCESTERSHIRE
    SAUCE
SALT AND FRESHLY GROUND BLACK
    PEPPER
25–50 G/1–2 OZ PARMESAN
    CHEESE, GRATED

SERVES 4

Remove the lettuce leaves from the stalks; use only the tender centre leaves for this salad, allowing about 10 leaves per person. Wash, dry and refrigerate until required.

To make the croûtons, stir the garlic into the oil and leave to infuse for as long as possible. Cut the bread into 5 mm/¼ inch cubes. Strain the oil into a frying pan over medium-high heat and quickly fry the bread cubes until they are an even golden colour. Drain on paper towels.

To prepare the Caesar dressing, plunge the eggs into boiling water, bring back to the boil and boil for 1 minute only. Break the eggs into a large salad bowl, scraping out the thin layer of cooked white. Gradually whisk in the oil, then the lemon juice, Worcestershire sauce, salt and pepper.

Add the lettuce leaves, croûtons and two-thirds of the cheese. Toss lightly. Pile on to four large plates, sprinkle with the remaining cheese and serve immediately.

TOMATOES AND MOZZARELLA
with pesto dressing

4–8 LARGE, WELL-FLAVOURED
  TOMATOES
325–450 G/12 OZ–1 LB BUFFALO
  MOZZARELLA CHEESE
225 G/8 OZ SMALL, MILD-
  FLAVOURED SALAD LEAVES
  (OAK LEAF, LAMBS' LETTUCE,
  LAND CRESS)
SALT AND COARSELY GROUND
  BLACK PEPPER
BASIL SPRIGS, TO GARNISH

PESTO DRESSING

50 G/2 OZ FRESH BASIL LEAVES,
  WASHED AND DRIED
1 LARGE GARLIC CLOVE, CRUSHED
50 G/2 OZ PINE NUTS
JUICE OF 1 SMALL LEMON
175 ML/6 FL OZ OLIVE OIL

SERVES 4

Wash and dry the tomatoes and cut into slices. Drain the mozzarella and cut into 5 mm/¼ inch slices. Wash and dry the salad leaves and refrigerate until required.

To make the pesto dressing, combine the basil leaves with the garlic, pine nuts and lemon juice in a liquidizer or food processor and blend to form a smooth paste. Gradually add the oil to make a thick sauce.

Arrange alternate slices of tomato and mozzarella around one side of four large plates, spoon on a little of the pesto dressing and sprinkle some salt and pepper over the cheese and tomatoes. Serve with the salad leaves and garnish with sprigs of basil.

TOASTED GOATS' CHEESE SALAD
with walnuts and creamy mustard dressing

225 G/8 OZ MIXED SALAD LEAVES
(CURLY ENDIVE, ROCKET,
LOLLO ROSSO, YOUNG SPINACH
LEAVES)

2 TOMATOES, SKINNED, SEEDED AND
DICED

SMALL BUNCH OF CHERVIL AND
TARRAGON

4 SMALL FIRM-TEXTURED GOATS'
CHEESES OR 325 G/12 OZ
GOAT'S CHEESE LOG, CUT INTO
4 SLICES

50 G/2 OZ BUTTER, SOFTENED

85 G/3 OZ WALNUT PIECES,
CHOPPED

4 SLICES OF FRENCH BREAD

MUSTARD DRESSING

5 TABLESPOONS WALNUT OIL

1 TABLESPOON WHOLE GRAIN
MUSTARD

½ TABLESPOON DIJON MUSTARD

1 GARLIC CLOVE, FINELY CHOPPED

2 TABLESPOONS RED WINE VINEGAR

1 TABLESPOON DOUBLE CREAM

GARNISH

2 TABLESPOONS BLACK POPPY SEEDS

2 TABLESPOONS FINELY CHOPPED
CHIVES

SERVES 4

Combine the salad leaves, diced
tomatoes and herbs in a large
bowl. Place all the ingredients for
the dressing in a screw-topped jar
and shake well to blend.

Place the cheeses on a baking
sheet, spread with the softened
butter and cover with the walnuts.
Cook under a very hot grill for
2–3 minutes or until evenly
browned and warmed through.
Toast the bread at the same time.

Pour a little dressing over the
salad leaves to moisten them. Toss
gently and arrange on one side of
four large plates. Set a piece of
toasted bread on the other side and
carefully lift the toasted cheese on
top. Drizzle a little of the
remaining dressing over the cheese.
Sprinkle with the poppy seeds and
chives and serve immediately.

CRISPY CHICKEN SALAD
with sesame seeds and chilli dressing

325 G/12 OZ MIXED SALAD LEAVES
  (CHICORY, ROCKET, LAMBS'
  LETTUCE, YOUNG SPINACH OR
  SORREL LEAVES)
4 SMALL CHICKEN BREASTS, ABOUT
  150 G/5 OZ EACH, CUT INTO
  STRIPS
50 G/2 OZ PLAIN FLOUR
1 EGG, BEATEN
125 G/4 OZ LIGHT SESAME SEEDS
VEGETABLE OIL FOR DEEP-FRYING
CORIANDER LEAVES, TO GARNISH

CHILLI DRESSING
125 ML/4 FL OZ SUNFLOWER OIL
2 TABLESPOONS SESAME OIL
3 TABLESPOONS RED WINE VINEGAR
2 GARLIC CLOVES, CRUSHED
3 TABLESPOONS SOY SAUCE
1 TEASPOON GROUND SICHUAN
  PEPPERCORNS
¼ TEASPOON MUSCOVADO SUGAR
½ TEASPOONS TABASCO SAUCE
2 TEASPOONS SWEET CHILLI
  SAUCE

SERVES 4

Wash and dry the salad leaves and refrigerate until required. Combine all the ingredients for the dressing, whisking well to blend.

Coat the chicken strips in the flour, then dip in the beaten egg and toss in the sesame seeds. Heat the oil to 190°C/375°F or until a cube of bread browns in 30 seconds. Deep-fry the chicken for 3 minutes or until golden brown. Drain on paper towels.

Toss the salad leaves in a little of the dressing and pile in the centre of four large plates. Arrange the chicken on top, sprinkle with a little more dressing and garnish with coriander leaves.

WILD MUSHROOM SALAD
with chicken

4 LIGHTLY COOKED CHICKEN
   BREAST FILLETS, SKINNED
225–275 G/8–10 OZ MIXED SALAD
   LEAVES (CURLY ENDIVE, LOLLO
   ROSSO, OAK LEAF, RADICCHIO)
2 TOMATOES, SKINNED, SEEDED AND
   FINELY DICED
50 G/2 OZ BABY SWEETCORN,
   LIGHTLY COOKED AND SLICED
   IN RINGS
100 ML/3½ FL OZ VINAIGRETTE
   (PAGE 29)
CHERVIL SPRIGS, TO GARNISH

MUSHROOM SALAD

85 G/3 OZ BUTTON MUSHROOMS
175 G/6 OZ MIXED WILD
   MUSHROOMS (CHANTERELLES,
   CEPS, TROMPET DE MORT,
   OYSTER MUSHROOMS)
50 G/2 OZ UNSALTED BUTTER
1 TABLESPOON OLIVE OIL
2 SHALLOTS, FINELY CHOPPED
2 GARLIC CLOVES, CRUSHED
2 TABLESPOONS SHERRY VINEGAR
3 TABLESPOONS FINELY CHOPPED
   CHERVIL
SALT AND FRESHLY GROUND BLACK
   PEPPER

SERVES 4

Cut the chicken across the fillet into 2 cm/¾ inch slices. Arrange on four large plates like the spokes of a wheel, leaving a space in the centre of the plate.

Combine the salad leaves, tomatoes and half the sweetcorn.

To make the mushroom salad, clean all the mushrooms, trim and cut into even-sized pieces. Fry in batches in the melted butter and oil with the shallots and garlic. Return all the mushrooms to the pan, add the sherry vinegar, fry quickly over medium-high heat, then stir in the chervil and season to taste with salt and pepper.

Toss the salad leaves in a little vinaigrette and pile in the centre of the chicken. Top with a layer of mushroom salad, then more salad leaves, and finish with mushrooms. Scatter any remaining mushrooms and sweetcorn between the chicken pieces, drizzle with vinaigrette, garnish with the chervil and serve immediately.

WARM CHICKEN LIVER SALAD
with bacon and new potatoes

225–275 G/8–10 OZ MIXED SALAD
    LEAVES (BATAVIA ENDIVE, OAK
    LEAF, LOLLO ROSSO, ROCKET)

16 TINY NEW POTATOES, SCRUBBED

175 G/6 OZ BACK BACON, CUT
    INTO THIN STRIPS

25 G/1 OZ UNSALTED BUTTER

1 SHALLOT, FINELY CHOPPED

450 G/1 LB CHICKEN LIVERS,
    TRIMMED, WASHED AND DRIED

100 ML/3½ FL OZ PORT

175 ML/6 FL OZ DOUBLE CREAM

1 TABLESPOON FINELY CHOPPED
    CHERVIL, TO GARNISH

HERB VINAIGRETTE

3 TABLESPOONS SHERRY VINEGAR

175 ML/6 FL OZ OLIVE OIL

SALT AND FRESHLY GROUND BLACK
    PEPPER

1 TABLESPOON FINELY CHOPPED
    CHERVIL

2 TABLESPOONS FINELY CHOPPED
    CHIVES

SERVES 4

Whisk together all the ingredients for the herb vinaigrette. Set aside. Wash and dry the salad leaves and refrigerate until required.

Boil the potatoes until just tender, drain and keep warm. Fry the bacon in a large frying pan until crisp, drain and keep warm. Add the butter to the pan and fry the shallot until soft. Increase the heat and fry the chicken livers for 1–2 minutes or until seared on all sides. Stir in the port, cream and salt and pepper to taste. Reduce the heat and simmer for a further 2 minutes.

Put the bacon and potatoes in a large salad bowl and moisten with a little of the herb vinaigrette; add the salad leaves and toss gently. Arrange the salad in the centre of four large plates. Remove the chicken livers from the pan with a slotted spoon, arrange on the salad and spoon over a little of the warm sauce. Sprinkle with the chervil and serve immediately.

BEEF TAPENADE

with watercress and lambs' lettuce

450 G/1 LB RARE ROAST BEEF, CUT
INTO 1 CM/½ INCH SLICES
1 LARGE RED AND GREEN PEPPER,
SEEDED AND CUT INTO 5 MM
X 5 CM/¼ X 2 INCH STRIPS
275 G/10 OZ WATERCRESS AND
LAMBS' LETTUCE
12 BLACK OLIVES, STONED
1 TEASPOON CAPERS, DRAINED

TAPENADE DRESSING

150 G/5 OZ BLACK OLIVES, STONED
50 G/1¼ OZ CANNED ANCHOVY
FILLETS, DRAINED AND RINSED
3 TABLESPOONS CAPERS, DRAINED
50 G/2 OZ CANNED TUNA, DRAINED
JUICE OF 1 SMALL LEMON
½ TEASPOON DIJON MUSTARD
4 TABLESPOONS OLIVE OIL
4 TABLESPOONS VINAIGRETTE
(PAGE 29)

HERB CROSTINI

2 TABLESPOONS OLIVE OIL
2 TABLESPOONS FINELY CHOPPED
PARSLEY, CHERVIL AND CHIVES
4 SLICES OF FRENCH BREAD,
ABOUT 2 CM/¾ INCH THICK

SERVES 4

To make the tapenade dressing, blend the olives, anchovies, capers, tuna, lemon juice and mustard to form a smooth paste. Gradually blend in the oil. Put 4–5 tablespoons of the tapenade paste into a large bowl (refrigerate the remainder for use in another dish). Add the vinaigrette and mix well. Stir in the beef and peppers, cover and refrigerate for a few hours before serving.

To make the herb crostini, preheat the oven to 200°C/400°F/ Gas Mark 6. Combine the oil and herbs and brush over the bread. Bake until crisp and golden.

Mix the watercress and lambs' lettuce and divide between four large plates. Set a crostini in the centre of each plate and arrange a pile of beef tapenade on top. Sprinkle the olives and capers over the salad and serve immediately.

MARINATED HERRING SALAD
with sour cream dressing

4 LARGE HERRINGS, GUTTED,
  BONED AND FILLETED
225 G/8 OZ MIXED SALAD LEAVES
3 TABLESPOONS VINAIGRETTE
8 SMALL POTATOES, COOKED AND
  SLICED
1 TABLESPOON FINELY CHOPPED
  CHIVES

MARINADE

150 ML/5 FL OZ CIDER VINEGAR
150 ML/5 FL OZ WATER
3 TABLESPOONS CASTER SUGAR
1 SMALL ONION, SLICED
2 BAY LEAVES
8 PEPPERCORNS
8 ALLSPICE BERRIES
FEW FENNEL STALKS

SOUR CREAM DRESSING

300 ML/10 FL OZ SOUR CREAM
1 SMALL RED ONION, QUARTERED
  AND THINLY SLICED
4 TABLESPOONS CHOPPED SPRING
  ONION
FRESHLY GROUND BLACK PEPPER

SERVES 4

Cut the herrings into 2.5 cm/
1 inch pieces and place in a large
glass bowl. Put all the ingredients
for the marinade into a saucepan,
bring to the boil, then simmer for
about 2 minutes. Leave until
completely cold. Pour the cold
marinade over the herrings, cover
and refrigerate overnight.

Mix all the ingredients for the
dressing in a large bowl. Drain the
herrings from the marinade, pat
dry and mix into the dressing.

Toss the salad leaves with the
vinaigrette and divide between
four large plates. Arrange the
potatoes on the plates in
overlapping slices. Pile the herrings
on top of the potatoes, sprinkle
with chives and serve immediately.

SPICY CABBAGE AND NOODLES
with warm scallops

12 SMALL SCALLOPS

125 G/4 OZ VERMICELLI NOODLES

3 TABLESPOONS SUNFLOWER OIL

1 LARGE ONION, THINLY SLICED

2 GARLIC CLOVES, CRUSHED

1 SMALL RED CHILLI, SEEDED AND
FINELY CHOPPED

8 THIN SLICES OF FRESH GINGER

2 LARGE RED PEPPERS, SEEDED AND
CUT INTO STRIPS

1 SMALL SAVOY CABBAGE,
QUARTERED, CORE REMOVED
AND FINELY SHREDDED

50 G/2 OZ BEANSPROUTS

3 TABLESPOONS CHOPPED
CORIANDER, PLUS EXTRA
TO GARNISH

SPICY DRESSING

6 TABLESPOONS SUNFLOWER OIL

2 TABLESPOONS SESAME OIL

2 GARLIC CLOVES, CRUSHED

4 TABLESPOONS RED WINE VINEGAR

4 TABLESPOONS TERIYAKI SAUCE

2 TABLESPOONS THAI FISH SAUCE

PINCH OF MUSCOVADO SUGAR

1–2 TEASPOONS SWEET CHILLI
SAUCE

SERVES 4

Place all the ingredients for the dressing in a screw-topped jar and shake well to blend.

Wash and trim the scallops and pat dry.

Cook the noodles according to the packet instructions, then drain. Heat 2 tablespoons of the oil in a wok and fry the onion, garlic, chilli and ginger until soft. Add the peppers, then the cabbage, tossing quickly until slightly wilted. Add the drained noodles and the beansprouts. Pour over the dressing, bring to the boil, then stir-fry for a few minutes. Stir in the coriander.

Brush each scallop with a little sunflower oil and sear on a very hot cast-iron pan for 30 seconds each side.

Pile the cabbage mixture on to four large plates and arrange the scallops on top. Garnish with coriander and serve immediately.

SMOKED SALMON SALAD
with potato cakes and sour cream

125 G/4 OZ LAMBS' LETTUCE

125 G/4 OZ ROCKET

85 G/3 OZ CHICORY, CUT INTO
SLIVERS

325 G/12 OZ SMOKED SALMON,
CUT INTO STRIPS

2 TOMATOES, SEEDED AND DICED

4 TABLESPOONS SOUR CREAM

8 CHIVES, TO GARNISH

POTATO CAKES

225 G/8 OZ COOKED, MASHED
POTATOES

25 G/1 OZ BUTTER, MELTED

50 G/2 OZ PLAIN FLOUR, PLUS
EXTRA FOR SHAPING AND
COOKING

LEMON DRESSING

6 TABLESPOONS OLIVE OIL

2–3 TABLESPOONS LEMON JUICE

SALT AND FRESHLY GROUND BLACK
PEPPER

2 TABLESPOONS CHOPPED CHIVES

SERVES 4

First make the potato cakes. Mix the potatoes, butter and flour together to form a light dough. Roll out on a lightly floured surface to about 2 cm/½ inch thick. Using a 6 cm/2½ inch round cutter, cut into four circles. Heat a large heavy frying pan, dust with a little flour and cook the potato cakes until lightly browned on each side. Remove from the pan and leave to cool.

Combine the salad leaves in a bowl. Whisk together the dressing ingredients and moisten the salad with 1–2 tablespoons.

Scatter the leaves over four large plates, set a potato cake in the centre of each and pile the salmon around the edge of the cakes. Arrange the tomato dice on the potato cakes, top with sour cream, garnish each with two strips of chives and finish with a dusting of freshly ground black pepper. Serve any extra dressing separately.

THE BASICS

TIPS AND TECHNIQUES

Allow 50–85 g/2–3 oz of salad leaves per person as the basis for a main course salad. This may appear to be rather a lot but once the leaves are dressed they lose some of their volume.

Some of the more delicate salad leaves such as lollo rosso and oak leaf wilt very quickly once picked – indeed they often look unusable. However, they can be revived by submerging in a large bowl of very cold water for 30–60 minutes before using.

When mixing a leaf salad, use a bowl about four times larger than the volume of leaves. This makes mixing, tossing and dressing much easier and gives better results.

Only toss salad leaves in their dressing minutes before serving, otherwise they will wilt and lose their crisp texture and fresh appearance. Salads of root vegetables, grains and pulses will improve in flavour if dressed several hours before serving.

To skin tomatoes, pierce the flower ends with the point of a knife and plunge, one at a time, into a pan of boiling water, enough to cover. Using a slotted spoon, constantly turn the tomato while counting to six. Remove from the pan and plunge into a bowl of iced water to stop the cooking. The skin should then peel off easily without tearing the flesh, which should still be smooth and firm.

VINAIGRETTE
(French dressing)

250 ML/8 FL OZ OLIVE OR
SUNFLOWER OIL
4 TABLESPOONS WINE VINEGAR, OR
LEMON OR LIME JUICE
1–2 TEASPOONS SALT
½ TEASPOON FRESHLY GROUND
BLACK PEPPER

**MAKES ABOUT 300 ML/
10 FL OZ**
Place all the ingredients in a
screw-topped jar and shake
vigorously until emulsified and
slightly thickened.

Larger quantities of vinaigrette can be made in a food processor. However, this should be done with care, as the vinaigrette can very easily become too thick, like mayonnaise.

Different combinations of oils and vinegars can be used as the basis for vinaigrette. Choose from oils such as soya bean, peanut, almond, hazelnut, walnut and sesame, and vinegars including cider, sherry, balsamic and those flavoured with herbs and fruit. Whichever you choose, remember to taste the dressing and adjust the proportions if necessary: it should be well balanced and delicate, to complement the food and not mask or overpower it. When using strongly flavoured oils such as sesame or walnut, use only a small amount and make up the volume with a blander-flavoured oil such as sunflower or corn.

Other ingredients such as mustard, garlic, herbs and spices can be added to this basic vinaigrette to give it individuality.

MAYONNAISE

2 EGG YOLKS
½ TEASPOON ENGLISH MUSTARD
POWDER
300 ML/10 FL OZ OLIVE OR
SUNFLOWER OIL
1–2 TABLESPOONS LEMON JUICE OR
WINE VINEGAR
SALT
PINCH OF WHITE PEPPER

MAKES ABOUT 300 ML/ 10 FL OZ

Put the egg yolks and mustard in a bowl and beat with a whisk – preferably electric – for 1–2 minutes or until pale and thick.

Begin adding the oil, drop by drop at first, whisking constantly so that the oil is absorbed. After a while the oil can be added in a thin steady stream – keep whisking as you add the oil.

When all the oil has been added and the mixture is very thick, taste and adjust the flavour with lemon juice or vinegar, salt and pepper. If it is too thick, stir in a little warm water.

Cover and store in the refrigerator for 3–4 days.

Mayonnaise can be made in a food processor; however, the recipe needs to be altered slightly and the result will be thinner and lighter.

Substitute a whole egg for one of the yolks. Blend with the mustard, then, with the machine running, add the oil in a thin steady stream. When the mixture thickens, scrape down the sides of the bowl, add the lemon juice or vinegar and season to taste.

THE MASTER CHEFS

SOUPS
ARABELLA BOXER

MEZE, TAPAS AND ANTIPASTI
AGLAIA KREMEZI

PASTA SAUCES
GORDON RAMSAY

RISOTTO
MICHELE SCICOLONE

SALADS
CLARE CONNERY

MEDITERRANEAN
ANTONY WORRALL THOMPSON

VEGETABLES
PAUL GAYLER

LUNCHES
ALASTAIR LITTLE

COOKING FOR TWO
RICHARD OLNEY

FISH
RICK STEIN

CHICKEN
BRUNO LOUBET

SUPPERS
VALENTINA HARRIS

THE MAIN COURSE
ROGER VERGÉ

ROASTS
JANEEN SARLIN

WILD FOOD
ROWLEY LEIGH

PACIFIC
JILL DUPLEIX

CURRIES
PAT CHAPMAN

HOT AND SPICY
PAUL AND JEANNE RANKIN

THAI
JACKI PASSMORE

CHINESE
YAN-KIT SO

VEGETARIAN
KAREN LEE

DESSERTS
MICHEL ROUX

CAKES
CAROLE WALTER

COOKIES
ELINOR KLIVANS

THE MASTER CHEFS

This edition produced for The Book People Ltd,
Hall Wood Avenue, Haydock, St Helens WA11 9UL
Text © copyright 1996 Clare Connery

Photographs © copyright 1996 Simon Wheeler

First published in 1996 by
WEIDENFELD & NICOLSON
THE ORION PUBLISHING GROUP
ORION HOUSE
5 UPPER ST MARTIN'S LANE
LONDON WC2H 9EA

British Library Cataloguing-in-Publication data
A catalogue record for this book is available
from the British Library.

ISBN 0 297 83633 1

DESIGNED BY THE SENATE
EDITOR MAGGIE RAMSAY
FOOD STYLIST JOY DAVIES